RUNNING

The Alex Decoteau Story

RUNNING

The Alex Decoteau Story

A Play in One Act
for Six Actors

By

Charlotte Cameron

FICTIVE
PRESS

2014

A FICTIVE PRESS Book

While the events described and some of the characters in the play may be based on actual historical events and real people, the play is a work of fiction.

First published in 2014 by Fictive Press, a division of BizNet Communications (2815699 Canada Inc.), British Columbia, Canada.

fictivepress.com

"Fictive Press" and "fictivepress.com" are trademarks of 2815699 Canada Inc.

Amateur rights: Playwrights Guild of Canada administers amateur rights (for schools, community groups and amateur theatre group). Details at http://www.playwrightsguild.ca/services-visitors

Professional rights: Contact fictive press at publish@fictivepress.com

Cover design by Fictive Press. Cover photo of Alex Decoteau (EA-10-2072), 1912, Alberta representative to the Stockholm Olympic Games (Photographer: Sanderson), and cover background photo (EA-10-3184) of Jasper Avenue businesses with World War I proclamations, August 3, 1914 , with permission from the City of Edmonton Archives. Author photo by Tom Cameron.

Library and Archives Canada Cataloguing in Publication

Cameron, Charlotte, author

Running: the Alex Decoteau story / by Charlotte Cameron.

"A Play in One Act for Six Actors."

Issued in print and electronic formats.

ISBN 978-1-927663-13-4 (pbk.).--ISBN 978-1-927663-14-1 (smashwords).--ISBN 978-1-927663-15-8 (kindle)

1. Decoteau, Alex, 1887-1917--Drama. 2. Runners (Sports)--Canada--Drama. 3. Soldiers--Canada--Drama. 4. Cree Indians--Canada--Drama. 5. One-act plays. I. Title.

PS8605.A4787R85 2014   C812'.6   C2014-903757-0

C2014-903758-9

For my husband, Tom Cameron, who put his heart and talents into the race to get this play up and running for its premiere production.

Contents

Foreword

Alex Decoteau died October 30, 1917, at the Battle of Passchendaele, serving with the 49th Battalion (Edmonton Regiment) in that unit's bloodiest 24 hours in the war.

Nearly a century ago it might have been supposed that, despite his remarkable record as an Edmonton athlete and police officer, his memory would soon be forgotten outside of his family and close friends, as were the vast majority of that war's dead. Charlotte Cameron's play, *Running*, has been an important part of a process begun five decades after his death, which has gradually restored general awareness of this remarkable man.

Decoteau was a champion long-distance runner who represented Canada at the 1912 Olympic Games. An alumnus of the infamous residential school system, he became the first aboriginal on a Canadian police force and advanced to the rank of sergeant. Had he so chosen, his employment could have honourably kept him out of the army in 1916. Instead, he decided to enlist—and over a year later fell in combat.

This meticulously researched play brings Alex Decoteau—the man, his life, his death—before us. A man of ability, ambition, and integrity. And at root: a true warrior. Homely details of a soldier's life at the front emerge, yet Cameron neither flinches from the horror of Decoteau's final time in combat nor wallows in it. The fatal quagmire of Passchendaele is portrayed dispassionately in matter-of-fact language and, indeed, partly through the actual words of some who endured it.

Running leaves us with a wistful awareness of the truth of historian Barbara Tuchman's 1962 comment that part of the lasting impact of the First World War came from "wiping out so many lives which would have been operative on the years that followed." Alex Decoteau was one such life.

—*Major (Retired) David Haas, CD, rmc, BA (Hons), MA, JD*

Introduction

Running: The Alex Decoteau Story is an act of imagination inspired by the life and times of a Canadian hero. So many stories had been told and retold by family and friends of Alex Decoteau that they have taken on a myth-like quality, but fact or legend, they are consistent. Alex Decoteau had many talents and he used them well. He was a real person with hopes, dreams and the determination to make them a reality. I am grateful to the community of family and friends of Alex Decoteau for keeping this story alive for our times.

Although on the surface it might appear that Alex Decoteau (pronounced Alec Dakota) had an easy life, in fact, it began and ended tragically. His father had taken up farming near Battleford, in what was then the Northwest Territories. When Alex was three years old, his father was murdered by a visiting American, who was subsequently convicted and imprisoned. His widowed mother returned to her home on the Red Pheasant Reserve, where she later remarried. Alex and his siblings had to go to residential school, the Battleford Industrial School for Indians. In 1900, when the children were forbidden to speak their own language in the school, Alex would have been twelve. Alex's mother spoke only Cree, and Alex loved his mother.

While at the school, Alex and other boys were coached in the game of soccer by Irish policemen. It's no surprise that his team went on to win a provincial championship.

Alex loved to run and after moving to Edmonton at the invitation of his sister, Emily, and her husband, David Latta, he became known as "The Tom Longboat of the West."

A 1995 visit to the City of Edmonton Police Headquarters introduced me to Alex Decoteau. In a small museum, I found a motorcycle similar to the one Alex rode as a police officer in 1915. I was moved to see Alex's school notebooks and personal effects, such as a pencil case he'd made while attending The Battleford Industrial School in what became the province of Saskatchewan in 1905. The pencil case was the old-fashioned type with a top compartment that swung open to reveal pencils in the lower compartment.

In storage was the Waltham watch, which had been presented to Alex Decoteau by King George V for winning a five-mile race when Alex was stationed in Witley, England. Alex cherished the watch and wore it for the rest of his short life. When he was killed by a sniper at the Battle of Passchendaele on October 30, 1917, it was in his pocket.

Like many others, I've never forgotten my introduction to Alex. I wanted everyone to know about him, and friends encouraged me to write his story as a play.

The original play

Running: The Alex Decoteau Story premiered at the Edmonton Fringe Theatre Festival in 2001. As it happened, a visit from the Earl and Countess of Wessex coincided with the Festival. Because of the story of the watch Alex had received from King George V, I was invited to a function held for the Royals in Edmonton. Upon learning, in answer to her question, that the watch was in storage in Edmonton, the Countess remarked that it should be on public display.

At the time, I was teaching at Eastwood School, roughly in the same area where Alex lived after he moved to Edmonton. The students were particularly interested in the fact that King George V had given Alex his own gold pocket watch instead of the usual trophy, which had been "lost in transit." This convenient expression worked its way into daily school life, so a child might explain that her missing running shoes had been "lost in transit."

The family version of the play

After the 2001 Edmonton Fringe Theatre Festival, I received encouragement from people who attended the play, especially from relatives of Alex Decoteau. I also learned more about Alex as I continued to stay in touch with those who had helped me in my research. David Ridley from Heritage Community Foundation (now defunct) offered help with resources for schools involved in the Alex Decoteau Run (see below). Subsequently, Heritage Community Foundation developed an Alex Decoteau website. I decided to write a second play to include new information for a family audience.

I received a generous grant from The Alberta Foundation for the Arts to write a new play for Edmonton's 100th Birthday Celebration on October 8, 2004. The play premiered at what is now the Art Gallery of Alberta. I collaborated with three actors from the original Fringe production, Trevor Duplessis, Amelia Maciejewski, Christine Sokaymoh Frederick, and the director, Laura Roald.

Trevor Duplessis, Amelia Maciejewski-Duplessis, Charity Principe and Dean McQuay took on the acting roles. Trevor Duplessis also wrote a song for the play, to music composed by Dean McQuay, which captured Alex's willingness to always do his best to help others. After Edmonton's 100th Birthday Celebration, we restaged the play at Alex Taylor School for a Remembrance Day Ceremony, where Izola Mottershead, Alex Decoteau's great niece, launched her biography, *before – Alex Decoteau – after.*

The City of Edmonton Archives gave us permission to show historic slides to introduce the play. Some of the images are included in this book. The Loyal Edmonton Regiment Military Museum loaned uniforms, and Major (Retired) David Haas provided invaluable research material related to the First World War.

The Alex Decoteau Run

Alex Decoteau Run, May 2002. Edmonton Journal/Candace Elliott

In 2000, my first play, *No Gun for Annie*, was staged at the Edmonton Fringe Theatre Festival. It recounted the story of Annie Jackson,

Edmonton's and Canada's first policewoman. Alex Decoteau, a colleague of Annie, was an anonymous character in that play, but I felt strongly that his story needed to be told all on its own. I was considering making a movie of Alex's story but a colleague suggested a run instead, and gave me the names of two aboriginal police officers from the Edmonton Police Service who might be interested in the project: Jim White and Sharon Bourque. They liked the idea, so we set up a meeting in the staffroom at Eastwood School. There wasn't an empty seat. Alex Decoteau's great niece and nephew , Izola Mottershead and Alex Latta, attended, as did others from the Edmonton Police Service, the Edmonton Public Schools and the City Centre Education Project, along with teachers, librarians and staff from other schools. Principal Paul Gish gave the go-ahead for the project.

The first Alex Decoteau Run was held on May 4, 2001, a date chosen to coincide with Education Week, in Rundle Park before it officially opened for the summer. There was still ice on the river but the weather was hot. About 500 students took part. Everyone loved it and we started planning for the following year. A few months later, in August, my play, *Running,* was staged at the Edmonton Fringe Theatre Festival to critical acclaim. It gave impetus to the Run, which took on a life of its own. For the next nine years, the Alex Decoteau Run averaged about 1,500 children of all ages, accompanied by running or cycling adults. We had opening prayers from Elders, guest speakers, and drumming and dancing from groups such as The White Buffalo Dancers and Drummers Society. Many sponsors, such as the Edmonton Police Service and Running Room Ltd., played a huge part in the successful operations of the Run.

We also organized an annual poster contest for school children. School bus trips "back in time" took us to places Alex would have known, including to the Loyal Edmonton Regiment Military Museum to view an Alex Decoteau display specially prepared by David Haas, the current director of exhibits.

The newest version of the play

In this published version of the play, the first six scenes are close to the original 2001 Fringe production. However, I have made changes to other scenes to make them more historically accurate, based on suggestions from relations of Alex Decoteau and others.

The Fringe Production

Running: The Alex Decoteau Story was performed by The High Level Bridge Players in the Walterdale Playhouse at the 2001 Edmonton Fringe Theatre Festival. The play ran from August 17 to August 26, to positive reviews:

> *"Clever staging and solid performances make for a well-told story in this brisk 50 minute play about an Edmonton hero who deserves to be better known."* (Marc Horton, Edmonton Journal, Aug. 11, 2001.)

> *"A true story. Cleverly staged and some fine performances."* (Judy Unwin, ITV.)

The venue

The play was performed on an apron stage, 22 ft. square, surrounded on three sides by risers for the audience. Upon arrival, the audience could observe all the props and costumes arranged on the stage for the entire production.

Sets, props and costumes

We used six square, flat-topped stools, 40 cm in height. Felt pads were glued to the feet of the stools so the actors could slide them around the stage.

Rehearsal: (from left) Kurt Spenrath, Trevor Duplessis, Charity Principe

About 30 burlap "sandbags," stuffed with shredded paper, were used for the flood and war scenes. Army jackets, helmets, a skirt, a newspaper and small props were placed on the sandbags, for use when needed.

Two rolls of black landscape fabric (geotextile) were used to represent the mud at the Battle of Passchendaele. Sprayed with yellow, red and brown paint, the landscape fabric covered the stage completely when unrolled. A gap between the two rolls of fabric let Alex sink to his death in the mud. This set garnered positive comments from reviewers.

Of special note were the three scrolls, each 10 feet by 10 inches, made of light canvas and used to variously represent a bridal veil, a bouquet, a camera, the finish line for races, letters, a nurse's uniform and pigeons flying into the sky.

Rehearsal: (left to right) Charity Principe, Kurt Spenrath, Trevor Duplessis and Amelia Maciejewski

The actors, dressed entirely in black, added skirts and army jackets as needed. An actor wore a shawl to depict Alex's mother. Two policemen's hats, army helmets and a whistle were also used. There was no curtain. Sound effects, music and lights signalled transitions. The actors sang such well-known tunes from The Great War as *Pack Up Your Troubles*, *Let Me Call You Sweetheart* and *It's a Long Way to Tipperary*.

Original cast and crew

Actor	Character
Trevor Duplessis	Alex Decoteau (pronounced "Alec Dakota")
Christine Frederick	Alex's mother, his sister Emily, voices
Amelia Maciejewski	Annie Jackson, voices
Charity Principe	Soldier, French girl, nurse, voices
Kurt Spenrath	Police Sergeant, soldier, commander
Joe Procyk	King George V, voices

Production Crew

Director	Laura Roald
Sets	Tom Cameron
Lighting and Sound	Laura Roald and Fringe technicians
Stage Manager	Laura Roald and Charlotte Cameron
Producer	Tom Cameron

Running: The Alex Decoteau Story

A Play in One Act for Six Actors
By Charlotte Cameron

Production Notes

Main characters (in order of appearance)

Alex Decoteau (1887-1917). Raised on the Red Pheasant Reserve in Saskatchewan, Alex Decoteau became Canada's first aboriginal policeman in 1911. He raced at the 1912 Olympics in Stockholm, and later served with Edmonton's 49th Battalion in England, France and Belgium from 1916 to 1917. He was killed by a sniper while running a message at the Battle of Passchendaele on October 30, 1917.

Emily Latta (née Decoteau), elder sister of Alex Decoteau, married to David Latta.

Mother of Alex Decoteau, known as Mrs. Dora Pambrun after she remarried following the death of her husband, Peter Decoteau.

Annie Jackson (1878-1959). Born in Ontario, Annie Jackson moved to Alberta in 1909, where she became a social worker at the Ruthenian Children's Shelter in Edmonton. She joined the Edmonton Police Service in 1912, becoming Canada's first policewoman.

King George V of England.

Lieutenant Colonel Palmer, Battalion Commander of the Canadian Expeditionary Force (CEF), as the army was called at the time.

Prime Minister Robert Borden, Canada's wartime Prime Minister from 1911-1920.

Secondary characters (in order of appearance)

Children on the Red Pheasant Reserve in Saskatchewan.

Newsboy.

Bonhag, a runner representing the U.S.A. at the 1912 Stockholm Olympics.

Photographer.

Voices.

Sergeant on the Edmonton Police Service.

Police Constables on the Edmonton Police Service.

Flood victim.

Woman at dance.

Man at dance.

Herbert Yenby, witness to Alex's Attestation Paper when he signed up to fight.

French girl.

Nurse.

Soldiers in the Canadian Expeditionary Force (CEF).

Officers in the CEF.

Props

The stage directions call for the following props:

6 square stools, sturdy enough for actors to sit or stand upon;

3 canvas scrolls, 10 feet long by 10 inches wide, used to represent multiple items, such as letters, a bridal veil, a nurse's uniform, a finish line, etc.;

30 burlap "sandbags" stuffed with shredded paper;

2 rolls of landscape fabric sprayed with yellow, red and brown paint to represent muddy fields;

Other props: pocket watch, helmets, policemen's hats, whistle, white feather.

Setting

Running moves through time, from 1893 to 1917, and takes place in multiple settings, in the following order:

The Red Pheasant Reserve in Saskatchewan, 1893 and 1908;

Edmonton, Alberta, from 1908 to 1917;

The Stockholm Olympics, 1912;

England, France and Belgium, 1916-1917;

Edmonton, Alberta, November 1917.

The first scene takes place on the Red Pheasant Reserve in Saskatchewan, from 1893 to 1908.

The middle section of the play (scenes 2 to 5) occurs after 1908 and is set in the heart of Edmonton, where Alex Decoteau walked a policeman's beat. Like other prairie cities a decade after the Klondike Gold Rush, Edmonton was booming as people from all over the world arrived to look for work. The Legislature building and the High Level Bridge were under construction. New neighbourhoods, schools and theatres were transforming the city. People thought the world was their oyster; everything was going their way. This euphoric atmosphere collapsed in 1914 with the outbreak of the First World War.

The last section (scenes 6 to 10) of the play describes Alex's experiences as a soldier in Europe, leading up to his participation in the tragic Battle of Passchendaele in Belgium.

The play ends with an **epilogue** following Alex Decoteau's death.

Scene 1: Leaving Home

The Red Pheasant Reserve, District of Saskatchewan, Northwest Territories, 1893.

Opening Pantomime

Alex Decoteau, as a child, enters upstage centre. He sits on a blanket, stage centre, and tries to tie his shoelaces. His sister, Emily, enters centre stage right and helps him. She then teaches him how to run. They are joined by laughing children (the other actors) for a game of tag.

Wedding music. Actors exit upstage right except for Alex, who sits on the blanket, stage centre. Emily returns, wearing one of the scrolls as a wedding veil, and holding another neatly folded scroll representing her bridal bouquet. She walks to Alex, who stands centre stage centre, now an adult. She kisses him as she passes her bouquet to him, which becomes a letter. Alex holds one end of the scroll.

As the scroll unfolds, Emily holds the other end. She stands on a stool centre stage left. Alex walks back and forth across the stage as he read's Emily's letter.

Alex: *Reading a letter from his sister, Emily.*

My Dear Brother,

I think you will like it here in Edmonton, on the beautiful banks of the North Saskatchewan River. It doesn't have the sand dunes we ran on as children, and you can't ford the river like we used to do at North Battleford, but it is the same river. I pick berries in the valley below our house. People call it the Latta Ravine, after David's family. It's beautiful. There are Saskatoon berries. Highbush cranberries. Rose hips.

Emily: *Standing on a stool, centre stage left, she continues to read her letter to Alex.*

Now that David and I are settled into married life, we'd like to invite you to come and live with us in Edmonton.

Alex: *Still reading his sister's letter.*

There is a future here. David says the city is growing so quickly…

Cheerful music, such as A Bicycle Built for Two. *The actor playing Emily dons a shawl to indicate that she had become Alex's mother. She walks downstage centre, carrying the stool she's been standing on. She sits downstage centre. Alex walks to her, excitedly holding the letter. Alex moves around the stage as he reads, stressing the parts he likes. He is trying to persuade his mother to let him go to Edmonton. She does not want to lose him.*

Alex: Mother! There's a letter from Emily. I'll read it to you.

To Mrs. Dora Pambrun,
from Emily Latta,
9135 Jasper Avenue, Edmonton, Alberta.

My Dear Brother, Alex,

We would like you to come and live with us in Edmonton. Our house is so big it makes me lonely for my family. David also wants you to join us. He needs you to help him in his blacksmith shop.

Mother: You can work in North Battleford. We have blacksmiths here.

Alex: *Still reading.*

Or you could work on the police force. David says the city is growing so quickly they'll soon need to double the size of the police service. You would be eligible because you're single and a fast runner. That's important because the cars are speeding down Jasper Avenue, and the police officers must chase after them, on foot. *Laughs.*

Mother: That's dangerous!

Alex: She's just joking mother.

Mother: It's a wild, bad life in Edmonton.

Alex: But Emily is lonely there. And she says it's the same river as here. And there are all the things you need for your good medicine. You could come too, Mother.

Mother: No. I don't think so. This is where we belong.

Alex: They need me there, mother.

Mother: I need you here. First your father was killed and I moved back to the Reserve. I married Mr. Pambrun. You children all had to go away to school. Then Emily moved to Edmonton. That was all right. She married David. She has a big fancy house. A piano. What would you have? Nothing.

Alex: I'd have lots.

Mother: Your head will be turned. You'll be too full of yourself.

Alex: I won't mother. I'll prove it to you.

Mother: You'll forget me. You'll forget all of us. Alfred will want to join you.

Alex: He won't. I know he'll want to stay with you. Every time I look at the river I'll think of you. Emily says you can see the river from her window, and below it is Lovers' Lane.

Mother: I knew it. It's a bad city. You cannot go.

Alex: All right, mother. If you want me to stay, I will. But, I'd write lots of letters. And come home to visit.

He kneels beside her stool. She weeps. He puts his arm around her.

Alex: Why would I want to go? With you here, the prettiest mother. I can stay. It's alright.

Mother: *Slowly.* You really have to go don't you?

Alex: I won't go, mother. You know that. If you want me to, I'll stay here with you. But imagine! Emily says there is a housing shortage and people are living in tents!

Mother: Go. Keep your sister company.

Alex: You want me to go? You think I should keep Emily company?

Mother: You have to go. I didn't expect it to happen so soon. This place is too small. You need more room.

Alex: You mean it? I can go?

They hug each other. Alex helps his mother up from the stool and walks her off, downstage left, carrying the stool. He returns to stand, centre stage, for Scene 2.

Scene 2: Life in the City

Edmonton, 1911. Music, such as A Bicycle Built for Two. *Meeting Annie Jackson. Leaving Edmonton for the Olympics. Edmonton is a bustling, booming city. There are sounds of horses, buggies, cars, bicycles, pedestrians, and honky-tonk piano music. Alex, wearing a policeman's cap, runs on the spot at centre stage centre. He has a whistle. He imagines what it would be like to race against Tom Longboat, the famous runner of the 1907 Boston Marathon.*

Alex: *To audience.* They call me "The Longboat of the West." I'd love to race against Tom Longboat. He's the famous winner of the 1907 Boston Marathon. He toured out here, but didn't stop in Edmonton or Fort Saskatchewan. I think I could have beat him even though he'd likely have said, "Son, when this race starts all you will see is my back."

Alex laughs and runs upstage right to upstage left, circling to down stage centre where he runs into Annie Jackson, who has entered from down stage right and is standing down stage centre, reading a newspaper.

Annie: Don't you policemen have anything better to do than run after those speeding cars?

Alex: Miss Jackson! Sorry! Sorry! It's my job. That's no excuse, but if I see a car going more than 15 miles an hour down Jasper Avenue I have to give the driver a ticket.

Annie: You should have a policeman clearing the way for you.

Alex: Annie, don't be angry. We're friends, right? I don't need anyone clearing the way for me. I know you've heard that at the *Calgary Herald* Christmas Road Races I run ahead to clear the way for the other athletes, and I still win all the cups.

Annie: And so modest. Yes, it's always in the papers, every Christmas.

Alex: Miss Jackson. You're always so serious. I know you Methodists don't dance, but surely you can laugh.

Annie: Well I admit I was interested when I heard that you won the big race in Fort Saskatchewan. Everyone was impressed.

Alex: Surprised you mean.

Annie: Have you ever lost a race?

Alex: Yes. Once. My leg was acting up. It slowed me down. But I was alright with it. You see, as it happened, the second prize was a violin and I came in second. *Pause.* My mother always loved that violin.

Fiddle Music.

Annie: I hear you're going to the Olympics?

Alex: I hope so, but I have to make the team first. There's only one spot left.

Annie: But you were the fastest in Montreal.

She shows him the newspaper.

Alex: They still aren't sure. Chandler didn't compete. He was sick for the last race and they think he's faster. Now I have to go back to Vancouver and race against him.

Annie: But everyone knows you're the best. You win every *Calgary Herald* Christmas Road Race and you have so many silver cups you give them away. I have confidence in you.

Alex: I just hope I can best him. I'd give anything to go to the Olympics. It's been a goal of mine. To be like Tom Longboat. Sure I want the personal glory, but it's more than winning. I love my country. I want to represent Canada.

Annie: When you do go, who will look after those speeding cars?

Alex: Maybe you could give it a try.

Annie: Constable Decoteau!

Alex: Mark my words, you do a lot for this city. Everyone has seen how hard you work at the Children's Shelter. And you do a good job speaking up for women in court. You could do even more on the police force.

Annie: Don't be silly. We women can't even vote!

Alex playfully puts his hat on her and gives her his whistle.

Alex: It's a new world. I'm talking about progress, Annie. Cars on the avenue. Streetcars, sewers, telephones. People are coming to the city from all over. It's not going to be long before we have women police officers. Listen, if I can do it, so can you.

Annie: But you're practically famous.

Alex: Practically!

Annie: And so humble. You make policing look like a picnic. *She twirls the whistle.*

Alex: Listen, I don't enjoy being on show any more than you do. I hear rumours they're considering hiring a woman constable. Sooner or later you'll be chasing cars too.

Sound of a car. Alex runs to centre stage right. The car's brakes squeal. Alex runs back for his whistle.

Annie: Be careful. It just missed you. *Calls after him.* Good-day Constable Decoteau. *Annie keeps the hat.*

***

Music indicates the transition to the Olympics in Stockholm. A short running sequence. Alex and another actor run from upstage centre to downstage centre. Annie and Emily stretch a scroll across the stage from centre stage right to centre stage left, to indicate the finish line. While this is happening, the Newsboy calls out the details of the race.

Newsboy: *Upstage centre, standing on a stool.* Extra! Stockholm! July 10th, 1912. In the first heat of the first round of the 5,000 metres flat race, Bonhag of the United

States won over Alex Decoteau of Canada. Decoteau came in second.

Alex crosses the finish line and shakes hands with Bonhag.

Newsboy: But On July 11th Decoteau had to quit the big race with a cramp. He finished well out of the medals.

Alex cramps down. The photographer and Emily fold up the scrolls and throw them up for ticker tape. Parade music. It is the Welcome Home Parade for Alex in Edmonton.

Alex: *Speaking to the photographer, who uses a scroll to represent a camera.* Yes. It's good to be home. No medal unfortunately. This leg of mine acts up. I came in second in the First Heat of the First Round of the 5,000 Metres Flat Race and so expected to win on the big day, but I had to quit with a cramp. I think because I changed my gait.

Photographer: Do you think you'd have won a medal if you'd entered a shorter race?

Alex: Possibly. Wow! I'm so glad I went. I had the time of my life, and now I'm looking forward to getting back in my uniform and going to work tomorrow.

***

Other actors move to join a crowd downstage centre, outside the police station where Annie Jackson has just been sworn in as Canada's first policewoman. She is off to the side, centre stage left, standing with Emily. The photographer takes pictures of her, using a scroll for a camera. At the same time, two actors, centre stage right, congratulate Alex.

Voice # 1: You are my son's hero. He can't stop talking about you.

Voice # 2: Welcome back. We're proud of you, Alex. The Welcome Home Parade can't begin to express our thanks. You have the potential to become Canada's finest marathon runner.

Voice # 1: You have a wonderful future ahead of you.

Alex: Thank you. I'm sorry I didn't bring home a gold.

Voice #1: But you went. You did your best.

Alex: Yes. That's true and that Welcome Home Parade was really something.

Photographer: What a scoop! Olympic hero returns to meet Canada's first policewoman. How about a picture with the lady constable? *The photographer leads Annie over to Alex at centre stage centre. Annie is prim and proper as the photographer makes a fuss about posing the two of them. Alex agrees with the photographer.*

Alex: Anything to oblige.

Annie: Really, this isn't necessary.

Alex: Oh but it is. Congratulations. I'm happy for you Annie. You're the first policewoman in Canada.

Annie: They say Los Angeles is the first in North America.

Alex: Too bad they didn't hire you sooner. Everyone knew we needed a woman on the force.

Annie: Unlike you I am not interested in records. I only hope that I can make a difference.

Alex: Don't be so modest. You've come a long way. Remember when I was assigned to accompany you to Lamont when you were doing children's work?

Annie: Of course I remember.

Alex: By train and then by sleigh to rescue an abandoned baby?

Annie: *Nods affirmatively.*

Alex: And then the return trip to Edmonton late that night. After we arrived at the Children's Shelter you stood with the baby in your arms, snowflakes like stars on your eyelashes. When the Ruthenian matron opened the door she thought you were another homeless woman begging for shelter for the night.

Annie: Please.

Alex: Don't talk then.

Annie: Oh I meant to say, "Congratulations." You did well.

Alex: No Olympic medal unfortunately. This leg of mine acts up and I caught some kind of a bug. It slowed me down.

Annie: I have heard that if you had entered a shorter race you would have won the gold.

Alex: Oh well. It's water under the bridge. But my

favourite race in Stockholm wasn't even an official one.

Annie: Really?

Alex: It was just somebody's wild idea at the last minute. They thought it would be interesting to have four Native runners compete in a demonstration event. Two Americans, Gibson and Thorpe. Two Canadians, Keeper and me.

Annie: Who won?

Alex: *Laughs.* I'll tell you sometime.

Alex exits centre stage left. Annie remains at centre with the photographer, who puts on the policeman's cap and becomes the Police Sergeant.

Scene 3: The World Is Our Oyster

A beautiful fall day in Edmonton, 1913. People are down by the river preparing for the official opening of the High Level Bridge, an engineering feat that stretches across the North Saskatchewan River. From the bridge there is a view of the almost completed Legislature building. Nestled below it is old Fort Edmonton. Annie is on duty, taking instruction from the Police Sergeant, centre stage right.

Sergeant: Miss Jackson. I want you to walk behind the crowd for the official opening of the bridge. We can't have a near disaster like we had when the top level opened. High Level Bridge indeed! It's a wonder no one fell off it with all the pushing, and the bridge not finished. It's going to be nothing but a nightmare for us to police and we're understaffed as usual. If someone falls off they can't say I didn't warn them. Constable Decoteau is here, but that's no help.

Annie: Why not?

Sergeant: They had to think of some way to control the crowd. So all the people will line up behind the officials to walk across the river. They've got this fool idea that Decoteau will race ahead of them, up the hill on the south side, then double back to the north side, run up the hill and back down, and pass the official dignitaries before they reach the other side. People are taking bets.

Annie: *Laughs.* Where do I place my wager?

Music in the distance. Annie stands alone on the bridge, downstage centre. Alex runs towards her from upstage left.
They talk, downstage centre.

Annie: Well, I knew I should have bet on you, Alex.

Alex: But you're not a betting woman are you, Annie? You know when I was running across the bridge I got to thinking. Why don't we get married? Then we could really make headlines. Picture it. The first woman policeman, sorry, woman police officer, and the first Native policeman in the Dominion get married!

Annie: Don't be silly. Women are lining up waiting for you to pop the question.

Alex: Annie, I'm not joking. Everything's going our way. Look at this city. Look at the Legislature building over there. The dome! Beautiful granite from Vancouver Island. Peskapoo sandstone from Calgary. The world is our oyster! All we have to do is seize the moment. Let's just walk into the police station and see if Sarge will marry us.

Annie: Alex, we have to talk.

Scene 4: War and the Flood of 1915

The First World War has begun. Sounds of typing and telegrams being sent. Newsboy shouting from upstage centre. Ominous music eases the audience into Scene 4 and the beginning of the war.

Newsboy: Extra, Extra. Read all about it.

Alex: *Grabbing a paper and reading it.* Great Britain has declared war on Germany. A lot of men want to join up. Pete Anderson is shutting down his brickyard in the river valley and leaving right away.

Annie: *Centre stage.* That's reckless! He has a wife and children. I don't like that look, Alex. You can't go. We need you here.

Alex: It won't last long. They say it'll be over by Christmas.

Sound of water rushing. Alex walks slowly to downstage centre. Speaking to audience.

Now it's summer and we have a flood on our hands.

Voices from two actors as police constables, who stand upstage centre. They punctuate their statements by pounding stools.

Voices: *Speaking to audience.* Ladies and Gentlemen, this flood is serious. You must not go back into your houses. We'll help you when the water goes down.

Alex: *Speaking to other police officers, centre stage.* The water keeps rising. Someone is going to drown if people don't get out of their houses. We have to evacuate everybody.

Constable #1: The flood happened so quickly. It's as if everyone is mesmerized by the water.

Constable #2: Did you see the way those wooden sidewalks are buckling?

Constable #1: They look like the roller coaster in Borden Park.

Alex: *Speaking to Annie.* Just the other day I rode my motorbike down to the valley to lock up the High Level Bridge. The river was as calm as can be. The pans of ice had all gone by.

Annie: It's the sudden heat wave in the mountains and now the rains that have changed everything. We have to convince people to stay out of their houses. *They move to centre stage right and start picking up sandbags and placing them upstage centre right.*

Flood victim: *Standing on a stool, downstage right.* Everything in my house is floating, except the stove.

Annie: Here. Let me help you. Just step into the boat while I hold it steady.

Alex: You'll be safe in the school. *Jokes.* All your neighbours are there. Uncle Johnny moved food in from his store. You'll have beans and ham for dinner tonight. And tomorrow, for a change, ham and beans.

Constables, upstage centre, shade their eyes to see what's happening.

Constable #1: The Low Level Bridge. Do you see what's

happening? They've backed two trains on the bridge to hold it down. One from the north side. One from the south.

Constable #2: They're loaded with coal. But maybe they'll be washed away too.

Annie: *To Alex.* If the bridge goes, the trains go.

Alex: Don't worry. I watched the trains from over on the High Level Bridge. They're sitting with steam up. They'll be able to get off the bridge if necessary. We don't call the trains "The Ever Young and Pulling" for nothing.

Annie: But people have to keep back from the river. The bank is slippery mud and the water is deep and swift.

Constables #1 and #2: They can do it. The two trains are holding down the bridge. Nine box cars behind each engine. The "Ever Young and Pulling" has come to the rescue.

Alex: And now the firemen are coming to hose the mud and debris out of the houses. Listen.

Actors pass sandbags to each other, piling them upstage centre as they sing the most popular song of The Great War: Let Me Call You Sweetheart, I'm in Love with You.

Voices: *Singing.* "Let me hear you whisper that you love me true. Keep the home fires burning in your eyes so blue. Then let me call you sweetheart, I'm in love with you."

The sandbags remain in place for the rest of the play.

Woman: I just got a letter from my husband. He's safe in a hospital in England.

***

Edmonton, July, 1915. Music. The official opening of the Hotel Macdonald in downtown Edmonton, one week after the flood. The hotel overlooks the river. Annie stands at centre stage centre. Alex enters from stage right.

Annie: It's good you're here Alex.

Alex: It looks like the whole city has turned out for the opening. Are you having fun?

Annie: All the men are smoking. I can barely breathe.

Alex: Let's step out on the terrace. I know you Methodists don't dance, but the music sounds nice and the view is beautiful.

Woman: *High-society demeanour as she dances, with a partner, upstage left.* Everyone is here!

Man: It's hard to imagine that just last week the river flooded.

Woman: Yes. I saw a barn floating down the river with a cow on the roof. *Laughs.* Now we're back to normal.

Man: Thank goodness we didn't lose the Low Level Bridge.

Woman: Luckily the trains held it down.

Man: *Waltzing to centre stage centre.* Oh. Constable Decoteau. You haven't gone to war?

Alex: I have a job here, Sir.

Woman: *Hands Alex a white feather.* But don't you feel guilty? So many of our good men have been killed?

Alex: Would you like to dance, Madam?

Woman: No thank you.

Alex: How about you, Miss Jackson?

Annie: Well, just this once. *She takes the feather from Alex. Puts it in her pocket.*

The man and woman walk to stools centre stage left and sit quietly. Alex dances Annie across to centre stage right so they can talk.

Alex: Thanks for coming to my rescue. I hate these functions.

Annie: I thought you liked talking to people.

Alex: Not when they give me white feathers and think I'm a coward for not going to fight.

Annie: No one thinks that. You are a police officer. You're needed here. We're even using newspaper reporters as undercover agents.

Alex: The thing is, I want to go, but it seems they aren't taking any more Indians. At least for now. It says N.A.I. beside my name. North American Indian.

Annie: I don't believe this. I heard that quite a few

Natives from southern Alberta went.

Alex: Yes. They signed up right away. But now the Militia Department has stopped encouraging us. I want to go. I'm a Canadian. My father was one of Chief Poundmaker's men. I come from a long line of warriors and hunters. I'm fast. I want to use my speed to save my country.

Alex: Alex, don't go.

Alex: I want to go as soon as they'll take me. I can't stay with all the other men leaving.

Annie: You can stay. You don't have to leave. You don't have to prove anything. We need you here. Everyone knows you are in charge of your own police station. You're a sergeant now.

Alex: But I got promoted on April 11th, 1914. Over a year ago. Before the war started. They won't expect me to stay. The Canadian Corps needs me.

Annie: Because they're short of men. So many have been killed.

Alex: Annie, will you keep the home fires burning? Will you wait for me? Will you marry me, before I go? I want to come back and stand with you on that little bridge by my house and look down at the river.

Annie: You know I can't. I can't promise.

Alex: I want to see the Latta Ravine in the spring with honeysuckles and lilacs. Caragana hedges. When the days start getting longer I want to play baseball with the kids on the corner. I want to play soccer with the children. I want to run with the children. I want to have a family of my own.

Annie: You are going. You think it's your duty to be a warrior. But I have a duty too. If I marry you, I have to quit my job. All the time you're away I'd be useless. I wanted this job desperately. I got it. Now I'm going to keep it. There are problems here too.

Alex: But Annie. You could help in other ways. You could do so much.

Annie: Knit and sew.

Alex: And write letters. Annie, please. *She shakes her head.* Then how about a ride on my motorbike? To lock up the bridge so those noisy hooligans can't joyride on it. I'll let you drive the bike, if you want. Picture it.

Annie weeps. They dance.

Scene 5: The Oath and Dreaming of Mother

The swearing in of Alexander Decoteau. War songs, such as The Maple Leaf Forever. *At centre stage centre, three actors wrap Alex in the scrolls, as follows: Voice #1 puts the first scroll over and around Alex while asking the first question; Voice #2 does the same with the second scroll and question; Voice #3, with the third. Then they tug Alex back and forth as they fire questions at him.*

Voice # 1: What is your surname?

Alex: Decoteau.

Voice # 2: What are your Christian names?

Alex: Alexander.

Voice # 3: Date of Birth?

Alex: November 19, 1887.

Voice # 1: Place of birth?

Alex: Battleford, Saskatchewan, Canada.

Voice # 2: Address at present?

Alex: Room One, University Apartments, Edmonton, Alberta.

Voice # 3: Date and place of Attestation?

Alex: 24th of April, 1916, Edmonton, Canada.

Voice # 1: Trade or calling?

Alex: Police Sergeant.

Voice # 2: Height?

Alex: 5 feet, 10 inches.

Voice # 3: Chest measurements?

All: Minimum, 37 inches. Maximum expansion, 40 inches.

Voice # 1: Complexion?

All: Clear.

Voice # 2: Eyes?

Alex: Brown.

Voice # 3: Hair?

Alex: Brown.

Voice # 1: Religion?

Alex: Church of England.

Voice #2: Physical development?

All: Good.

Alex: Just good!

Voice # 1: Smallpox marks? Check.

Voice # 2: Vaccination marks? One, left.

Voice # 3: When?

Alex: As a child.

Voice # 1: Marks indicating congenital peculiarities or previous disease?

Voice # 2: Check.

Voice # 3: Slight defects not sufficient to cause rejection?

Voice # 1: Tattoo on left arm.

Voice # 2: Are you willing to be vaccinated or re-vaccinated and inoculated?

Alex: Yes.

All: Vaccinated. Anti-typhoid. Tetanum. Dysentery. *Give him shots.*

Voice # 3: Are you married?

Alex: No.

Voice # 1: Next of Kin?

Alex: Pambrun, Mrs. Dora. Mother, Battleford, Saskatchewan.

All: Are you willing to be attested to serve in the Canadian Over-Seas Expeditionary Force?

Alex: Yes. I, Alexander Decoteau, do solemnly declare that the above are answers made by me to the above questions and that they are true, and that I am willing to fulfil the engagements by me now made, and I hereby engage and agree to serve in the Canadian Over-Seas Expeditionary Force, and to be attached to any arm of the service therein, for the term of one year, or during the war now existing between Great Britain and Germany should that war last longer than one year, and for six months after the termination of that war provided His Majesty should so long require my services, or until legally discharged.

Voice #2: Date?

Alex: 24th April 1916.

Voice # 3: Witness?

Herbert Yenby: Herbert Yenby.

Voice #1: Now swear on the Bible.

Alex: I Alexander Decoteau, Do make Oath that I will be faithful and bear true Allegiance to His Majesty King George the Fifth, His Heirs and Successors, and that I will as in duty bound, honestly and faithfully defend his Majesty, His Heirs and Successors, in Person, Crown and Dignity, against all enemies and will observe and obey all orders of His Majesty, His Heirs and Successors, and of all the Generals and Officers set over me. So help me God.

Voice # 2: Sign here.

Alex and Herbert Yenby sign, then the actors unwind Alex from the scrolls. They let the scrolls fall downstage centre.

Voice # 3: Off to war you go.

Voice # 1: And this time you better win!

All: Regiment # 231462, Rank, Private. Joined on enlistment. 202 Sportsman's Battalion.

Sound of drums and marching.

***

Alex writes a letter to Emily using a scroll as paper. Emily holds the other end of the scroll.

Alex: Sarcee Camp, Calgary, October 4th, 1916.

My Dear Sister,

I don't know what they are going to do with us yet. Nobody knows for that matter. I wish I could find out. I was wondering if Mother could come up to Edmonton for a few days if I send her the money to pay her expenses. It would require almost a week's leave for me to go to Battleford and I'm almost certain that I can't get a week's leave. I may be able to get three days. I could easily come up and see you both in that time. If I was sure we were going to stay in Canada for the winter, I wouldn't worry because I could get a longer leave. I wish you would write me as soon as you get this letter and say whether it would be advisable or not to send for her.

I can't write you much more tonight Sis, as I'm not a bit too warm. Some nights we have to sleep with our clothes on. They have issued two more blankets to each man, but I was on duty in town yesterday, and so did not get mine yet. We bought an oil stove for our tent the other day but it costs too much to keep it going all night so it keeps me busy nights rolling over trying to dodge Jack Frost.

Emily: *Reading.*

Well, Sis, remember me to Dave and the children. I do hope to see you all before long, if only for a little while. Be good to yourself and don't work too hard.

As ever,

Your loving brother, Alex.

***

Transition to a dream. Drumming and chanting. Alex visits his mother. She mimes the application of war paint to his face. Alex and his mother are spot lit, downstage centre. The other actors stand upstage centre, behind them in shadow. They speak from the darkness while Alex's mother applies the paint.

Voice #1: Alex loved to run. He could run as many as four races in one day. In Lethbridge, he ran the ten-mile, five-mile, two-mile and the one-mile race. And won them all on the same day.

Voice #2: In 1912 Alex could run the mile in 4 minutes, 31 seconds. Forty years later, the runner, Roger Bannister, broke the four-minute mile. If Alex had trained for the one-mile event, he could have broken this record before 1915.

Voice # 3: From Halifax per S.S. Mauritania November 23, 1916. Arrived Liverpool, England, November 30, 1916.

Scene 6: Meeting the King

Transition to Europe, 1916. Music. Alex picks up the scrolls used in the swearing-in scene. He sits on a stool, downstage centre. Writes letters to Emily and Annie, who have picked up their end of the scrolls. At first the letters are cheery, but gradually become more depressing.

Alex: *Downstage centre. Writing on a scroll.*

Dear Annie,

December 1916. I have cheery news. Pete Anderson is the first Canadian to escape from a German Prison of War Camp. His buddies helped him. He hid in a well and then made it all the way to Denmark. He was back in England at the first possible date for an audience with the King.

Annie: *Downstage right. Standing on stool, holding one end of the scroll representing Alex's letter, she reads his letter.*

I too had an audience with the King. I know you'll laugh at that and say I am being immodest, but this is what happened. When I was in England, I ran in a race at Aldershot, which was hosted by King George the Fifth as part of a plan to boost the morale of the troops. When I won and stood before the King to receive my trophy, I got the surprise of my life.

Music. God Save the King. King George V enters from upstage centre and stands centre stage centre. Alex stands before him.

King: I apologize. I like to have everything in order. The trophy has been lost in transit.

Alex: That's understandable, Your Majesty. In times like these.

King: But we must give you something, young man. I heard you competed at the Olympics in Stockholm. I heard you can run a mile in 4 minutes, 31 seconds. And now you have won a five-mile race, but there is no reward.

Alex: Your Majesty. Meeting you is reward enough.

King: Oh dear. We must give you something. *The King pulls his gold watch out of his pocket.*

Alex: Oh no, Your Majesty. Your subjects know that you are very punctual.

King: Take it, my boy. I have others. Time is ticking away. And God bless you.

Annie: *Reading.*

The King took his own watch out of his pocket and gave it to me. It's a Waltham watch and I carry it with me at all times. It is in my breast pocket, along with your picture.

Your friend,
Alex.

Music. A village in France. 1917. Alex and two other soldiers are sitting, upstage centre, on sandbags. They listen to a French girl singing It's a Long Way to Tipperary.

French girl: *Centre stage left, singing.*

Alex: *Moves to centre stage. Sits on a stool, picks up the scroll that Emily is still holding and writes her a letter. The second scroll lies at his feet.*

The French people at whose barn we were billeted, used me very nice. They used to feed me on fresh eggs. If I didn't have a girl in Canada, I'd have certainly fallen in love with the oldest girl. She wasn't much on looks, but she was a good girl, and a worker.

French girl: *Continues singing.*

Emily: *Sitting on a stool, centre stage left, reading the scroll of Alex's letter.*

It's terrible to see that there are lots who suffer from shell shock or nervous breakdown, and they can't fight against fear, but most of the boys have a keen sense of humour and laugh at almost anything. Then we have our sports and games, concerts and picture shows where one may forget his troubles awhile.

Annie: *Writing on her end of the scroll. Alex picks up his end of the scroll (lying at his feet) as Annie begins to speak.*

I'm glad you are in good spirits. It is good to know that

there was a sports meet in the vicinity of Allouage northwest of Bruay. I have found it on a map of Belgium that I study on my kitchen table. Good for you to have placed first in a one-mile race on August 11th. You must be in good condition. You were truly modest about such an accomplishment! I know so little of where you are and what you're doing.

Emily: *Reading.* France, September 10, 1917.

My Dear Sister,

Received your very welcome letter yesterday and was very glad to know that you were all well. I also received the parcel some time ago and you may be sure the contents were very welcome. The tobacco came in handy as I was broke and without tobacco. I should have written at once and thanked you, but I was very busy at the time and kept putting it off. Then I was taken ill with trench-fever, and didn't leave my bed for ten days. I am about over it now, though my legs still pain at times, especially during wet weather. It's just like rheumatism and many a sleepless night I had to put up with. I was in bed most of the time while we were on Divisional Rest.

Alex: *Continues writing his letter to Emily.*

I have met quite a lot of Edmonton men since I came to France. We do such a lot of moving about, that we run across someone we know almost every day. I've met Frank Walker of Fort Saskatchewan several times and he always stops to shake hands, and do you remember Harry

Higgins? Brother of Maria. I met him in England. He was a sergeant in the 128th Battalion. I don't know if he is over here yet or not. I met Tom Longboat in England too. Dave McCullough is over here too. I see him every once in a while. It sometimes seems as if Edmonton has moved over here and left all the womenfolk behind, one meets so many from home. Every once in a while someone would come up to me and say, "Do you remember the time you chased me on your motorcycle?" Many an hour we pass away talking of old times and wishing we were all back home again.

The French girl gathers the two scrolls and puts them on to create a nurse's costume.

Scene 7: The Horror of War

France, September 10th, 1917.

Nurse: *Downstage centre, wearing scrolls as her uniform. Speaking to audience.* One horrible day, the first gassed patients were carried in. These were pitiful cases. There were many Canadian boys among them. This was an entirely new kind of warfare. It was awful. We didn't know how to treat them or give relief. Even oxygen was of little help. Most of the men were gasping for breath from the searing of their throats and lungs. It was a terrible experience for the men and for those of us trying to help them.

The nurse removes her scroll costume and carries one end of the scroll to Alex (centre stage) and the other end to Emily (centre stage left).

Alex: *Writing on the scroll.*

Dear Sis,

   I had a tough day the day before yesterday. I don't know whether it was the gas that sickened me or the berries that I ate. Some of the gas that "Fritz" is using now does not affect one till about 24 hours after. I was taken ill while on the march with vomiting, and later "sapoosowin" very severe. I wasn't able to hold down anything for two meals after. However I'm completely over it now, so there's nothing to worry about.

Emily: *Reading her end of the scroll.*

   But best of all for cheering a soldier's heart is a letter

from "Home." There's always a scramble when the mail is given out. Yes, and there's hardly ever a vacant desk at the Y.M.C.A. writing room. Letter writing is sometimes very difficult. A soldier loses his pack and with it his writing material. Maybe his pack gets soaked with rain, spoiling his papers and the nearest Y.M.C.A. is in the next town. He puts his writing off till a better time which does not turn up before he goes to the front line. A week or two slips by before he is able to write a letter.

Alex: *Continues writing his letter to Emily.*

We are grateful when there is mail from home. Julia told me about Jessie thinking of going to the hospital to nurse. It's a noble profession, but I'm glad she's not taking it up. It's a thankless job. Just like soldiering.

Annie: *Writes to Alex on a scroll.*

Yesterday the paper pasted up the longest list of casualties since the war began.

Alex: *Continues writing his letter to Emily.*

I am laying on the ground trying to finish this letter before dark. I hope I do for I don't know when I'll have another opportunity. I wish mother understood English and could read. I can't think of anything that would interest her, and she always complains that we write such short letters. It's the people who read our letters to her who are to blame. Don't tell her that I was sick when you write, Sis. It won't hurt her not to know.

Emily: *Reading Alex's letter on the scroll.*

Well Sis, in spite of the fact that we are used very decently by the French people, there's no use denying the fact that we are all aching and longing for our own beloved Canada. Of course there's work to be done yet and I spose I will stay here till it is finished. A man has lots of time to think of his people and home out here, and one does get awfully lonesome at times.

Annie: *Still writing her letter to Alex.*

You must take care of yourself.

Emily: I wish I could see you again.

Alex: *Writing.*

Well Sis, I don't know what else to tell you so I better close now. I'm enclosing a picture taken just after my attack while we were out on rest.

Speaking to audience. What a long war this is. It's difficult to have lived so long through it when everyone else is dead.

Emily, Annie and Nurse gather up the scrolls. Stand upstage centre with their backs to the audience. The nurse becomes soldier #3. Transition music.

***

Annie and Emily sing a slow, mournful Pack Up Your Troubles, *as Alex and two actors walk downstage centre. The soldiers are in a camp in Belgium, in October 1917. They know they will be going into battle soon. They sit on the ground, on the two pieces of landscaping fabric arranged to form a large, round water hole. They are washing and shaving and talking to each other.*

Soldier #1: Boy, it's been a miserable few days. You don't know whether you're going to step on a piece of mud or a bloated rat or what is going to be under the water.

Soldier #2: And now we're in a shell hole. I wish it would stop raining.

Soldier #3: My foot touched something. There are dead animals in this water.

Soldier #1: Don't say it.

Soldier #2: Yesterday we were under fire. Tomorrow we go up to the trenches.

Alex: Don't think about it.

Soldier #3: Who do you miss the most?

Alex: My family. My mother. My sister, Emily, my sweetheart.

Soldier #1: A sweetheart?

Alex: Yes. *Passes a picture.* This is her picture.

Soldier #2: You still love her?

Soldier #1: Let me see it. *Whistles.* Why wouldn't he love her? She's a beauty.

Soldier #2: What is your best memory?

Alex: I have so many good memories. But right now, because of the way my leg is giving me trouble, I think of the Olympics. My leg hurt then too, maybe that's why I think of it. I think of Tom Longboat. He was at the Olympics before me, but I met him in England when we were running races for the King. Tom's here in France, somewhere. And I think of the Americans, Gibson and Thorpe.

Soldier #3: You knew him? Jim Thorpe? What was he like?

Alex: He was the greatest athlete in the world. We raced together at the Olympics.

Soldier #1: I've never heard this.

Alex: It was a demonstration event. Someone got the idea that the four Native runners should race against each other. Thorpe, Gibson, Keeper and me.

Soldier #2: Who won?

Alex: We crossed the line together! *Stands. Raises his arms and laughs.* I wonder what Tom Longboat thinks about these days. I'll ask him when we get home.

Soldier #3: If we get home.

Soldier #1: You'll really be a hero.

Alex: We'll all be heroes. When we get home. *He takes out the King's pocket watch.*

Soldier #2: Can I hold it again? *Alex passes him the watch.*

Scene 8: This Is Not Going to Be a Picnic

October 25, 1917. Sound of guns. Passchendaele, Belgium. Soldiers spread the landscape fabric to cover the stage to represent a field of mud. The soldiers then stand downstage to deliver their lines; the officers, upstage.

Soldier #1: This is not going to be a picnic. The rains have made these lowlands a swamp of mud.

Soldier #2: How far do we have to go?

Alex: One thousand yards.

Soldier #3: One thousand deaths.

Soldier #1: The mud is so bad. It's the battle of the mud.

Alex: It takes four minutes to plough through fifty yards of mud.

Officer #1: *Banging a stool, turning and speaking to the soldiers.* I will not let you go until everything is ready.

Soldier #2: The first objective is the hill with a ruined village on top.

Soldier #3: The name of the village is Passchendaele.

Officer #2: *Banging stool.* Passchendaele! Let the Germans keep it. It must be a mistake. It isn't worth a drop of blood.

Soldier #1: Why do we have to do it?

Alex: We have to do it, that's why.

Alex and the soldiers talk to each other. They speak rapidly.

Soldier #2: *Speaking to audience.* There's no point to the battle of the mud at Passchendaele.

Officer #1: The point of the battle of the mud at Passchendaele is inexplicable. But Haig, the British Field Commander, is determined to take it and Palmer has to obey orders.

Alex: *Speaking to audience.* The Australians tried to take it. The British tried to take it and now they've called on the Canadians.

Soldier #3: *Stands beside Alex. Speaking to audience.* We have to take it before we ever get out of here.

Alex: *Speaking to audience.* The front line. There is no front line, just little shell holes, pockets in this mud. You've never seen such mud. And pools of water.

Soldier #1: *Kneels, miming digging action.* As fast as we dig one shovelful of mud out, two roll in.

Soldier #2: I've never seen a German at Passchendaele.

Alex: *Speaking to audience.* It's a slow advance in the mud. It is soupy you see, and really muddy. And when they shell us while we are making the attack these shells are dropping in the mud and not exploding. It is just so muddy.

Officer #2: Patrolling is not extensively carried out during the night. The men are very tired, but dig well.

Soldier #3: We put small semi-waterproof sacks over the muzzles of the rifles.

Soldier #1: Sometimes we use old socks.

Soldier #2: The dugouts are full of wounded men. A lot of men die in the dug-outs.

Officer#1: Some men have to lie outside. That can be luck because they are first to be picked up by the horse-drawn ambulances.

Alex: Quite a few of the stretcher-bearers never make it back because the road is always under fire. I've seen several stretchers and their bearers fall off the duck boards and drown.

Soldier#3: Stretcher cases, which normally require two bearers, now need as many as sixteen to get to the nearest first-aid station.

Alex: It is heavy going. There is no question about that. The sandbags are heavy to carry.

Scene 9: The Battle of Passchendaele

Alex sits on stool, centre stage, with his back to the audience. Palmer is downstage left. Three officers speak to the audience from upstage.

Officer#1: *He bangs down a stool.* The battle will be fought in three stages. Between each assault during a pause of several days, guns will be dragged to provide the next wave of troops.

Palmer: *Writing on a scroll folded up to resemble a journal.*

5:15 A.M. Runner from Advanced Report Centre reported assembly complete.

All: Zero hour is set for 5:40 A.M.

Alex: *Struggling to walk, speaking to audience.* I will not be running today. It will be more like swimming in a grey porridge of mud and blood. I am losing strength. Men are dying slowly. I hear them cry, but I cannot help. I try to breathe, then I see a red lung in the mud, with the windpipe still attached. My legs are useless.

Sound of a gunshot. Alex falls, separates the landscape fabric and slips in under the mud.

Officer #2: October 30 dawned shrouded with fog. A local creek is in flood, splitting the attack. On one side of the creek, Calgary's 50th Battalion, following Saskatchewan's 46th.

Palmer: *Still writing.*

5:54 A.M. The enemy shelling steadily increased in intensity and, directed by a plane, came down on the line of my men.

Officer #3: Edmonton's 49th was encountering fierce resistance.

Palmer: *Still writing.*

Furthest left, over in 5th Canadian Mounted Rifles, Major George Pearkes sent carrier pigeons asking for ammunition and relief.

The actors, standing upstage, unfurl three scrolls to represent carrier pigeons.

Scene 10: Killed In Action

Edmonton, November 10, 1917. Street noises. A newsboy pastes up a list of the war dead on the wall of a cigar store. The crowd gathers around to read the names. Emily and Annie stand centre stage centre. The people talk to each other about Alex.

Newsboy: *Standing on a stool, upstage centre.* Extra! Extra!

Voice #1: *Speaking to Voice #2.* They got Alex.

Voice #2: Alex Decoteau was my hero.

Newsboy: Alex Decoteau killed in the Field of Belgium at the Battle of Passchendaele. By a sniper's bullet. On October 30, 1917.

Emily: *Speaking to Annie.* Killed in Action on October 30th, 1917, in Belgium.

Annie: *Speaking to Emily.* Here it is November 10th, and he's been dead for eleven days. Oh Emily, I am so sorry.

Emily: We will never forget him. He was my brother.

Annie: He was my friend.

All: He was a runner.

Closing Pantomime

All the actors, except Alex, stand facing the audience in the same configuration as in the opening scene when Emily taught Alex how to run.

Alex stands up from the mud. The other actors pull the landscape fabric off to the sides of the stage. Alex runs on the spot. Then he runs all around the stage, joyfully tapping the other actors on the shoulder as in the opening scene. Then he runs to upstage centre where he jumps over the sandbags and exits. There are sounds of cheering. His life ends with a memory of crossing the finish line at the Olympics.

Palmer: *Writing on a folded scroll.*

Communication Report.

Owing to the formation of the ground, the use of visual signalling from Advanced Battalion Headquarters to Rear Headquarters was impossible. Three laddered routes were laid to an Advanced Report Centre but none of these lasted any time and communication by wire was ineffective during the day beyond Battalion Headquarters. All communications had to be made by runners.

Emily: *Reading a letter from Alex on a scroll.*

Give my love to Grannie when you see her. Love to the children. Remember me to what few friends I've left.

For yourself, good wishes, love and affection, from your brother, Alex.

Epilogue

Emily and Annie sing a verse of a beautiful sad song, such as Let Me Call You Sweetheart.

Prime Minister Borden: *Downstage centre. Speaking to audience.* Lloyd George, it is a great honour and privilege for me to come over to London and participate in this Imperial War Conference. There is though one thing I want to say which need not appear in the official record, Mr. Prime Minister. I want to tell you that, if there is a repetition of the Battle of Passchendaele, not a Canadian soldier will leave the shores of Canada so long as the Canadian people entrust the government of their country to my hands.

Emily and Annie sing another verse of the song.

Blackout.

Historical Note

The King's Pocket Watch*

In Aldershot, England, Private Alex Decoteau stood proudly as King George V presented him with his prize. It was 1916, four years after Decoteau had raced for Canada in the Stockholm Olympics and almost nine months since he'd enlisted to fight the Germans. While stationed in England, he took part in a military sports day, winning the five-mile foot race. When the trophy was discovered to be lost in transit, the King spontaneously proffered his own gold pocket watch instead. Alex treasured the King's pocket watch and carried it with him when he was transferred to the front in Belgium.

Decoteau was born in 1887 and grew up on the Red Pheasant Reserve near North Battleford in what was then the District of Saskatchewan, Northwest Territories. (Saskatchewan became a province in 1905.) His mother, Mary Wuttunee, was a daughter of the reserve's chief. His father, Peter, fought with Poundmaker's warriors at the battle of Cut Knife Hill on May 2, 1885, during the Northwest Rebellion, and afterward took up farming near Battleford. When Decoteau was three, his father was murdered by an American hired hand from a nearby farm, prompting his mother to move back to the Red Pheasant Reserve to raise her five fatherless children. In one of those twists of fate, David Latta, the Northwest Mounted Police officer who investigated Peter Decoteau's murder, married Alex Decoteau's aunt. After she died, Latta married Decoteau's sister, Emily, in 1900. In 1908 Decoteau left the Reserve to live with Emily and David Latta in their beautiful house in Edmonton.

Decoteau loved to run. He competed in every significant race in Alberta from 1909 to 1916 and usually won. By 1910, this Cree athlete had gained a reputation as the "Tom Longboat of the West," a reference to the legendary runner from the Six Nations Reserve in Ontario.

Alex Decoteau became Canada's first aboriginal policeman when he joined the Edmonton force in 1911. As an Edmonton police officer, one

---

* Much of this material was first published in "The Running Warrior," an article by Charlotte Cameron published in the June-July 2013 issue of *Canada's History*.

of his jobs was to patrol the bars of Edmonton. Another was to catch cars speeding down Jasper Avenue. If he saw one going over 15 miles per hour, he pursued the vehicle on foot and ticketed the driver. No one seemed to hold it against him. A few years later, when serving in the army in Europe, Edmonton soldiers would shake his hand and ask if he remembered chasing them.

The 1912 Olympic Games were a high point in Decoteau's life. When he sailed on the Teutonic to compete in Stockholm, he was full of hope and wired his family that he would "endeavour to bring the bacon home to sunny Alberta." Decoteau had worked hard to make the Olympic team, competing in trials in Fort Saskatchewan, Toronto and Montreal. He expected to win the 10,000 metre race in Montreal, but as he tried to pass Joe Keeper he got a cramp and quit at the fourth mile. He then entered the 5,000 metre race and won, beating the British Columbia champion, W.R. Chandler. Decoteau and Keeper were sent to Sweden to represent Canada.

Although considered to be a dangerous contender, Decoteau didn't place in the 5,000 metre race in Stockholm. He received a Participant's Medal and an Olympic Merit Certificate, and returned home to a hero's welcome in Edmonton, where he was very popular. There were several aboriginal athletes at the games and the Swedish press persuaded them to put on an exhibition race. They all crossed the finish line together. When Decoteau was asked if they'd planned it, he said, "Heck no, we're all from different tribes."

One of Decoteau's favourite races was the annual *Calgary Herald* Christmas Day Road Race. It was 6.2 miles long and often gruelling because of the cold and snow. He broke the record in 1910, and then his own record in 1914 and 1915. He wore a balaclava, which he folded up for the benefit of the 20,000 spectators, and he enjoyed clearing the road of cars to give the runners behind him a chance. A referee described him as deserving of the "cheers which greeted him as the best distance man in Alberta." He had his heart set on keeping the trophy for good but needed to win the race three years in row. He wasn't able to run the 1916 race because he had enlisted to fight in the First World War in April 1916 — until the end of 1915, the Canadian Corps would not accept aboriginal volunteers. After arriving in England in November 1916, he tried to convince the race organizers in Calgary to let him race against the clock instead. They refused and he didn't live to learn that his family received the cup in his honour.

Decoteau became a runner in France and Belgium, relaying messages up and down the line, and always carried the King's gold pocket watch. He had it on him in October 30, 1917 when he was killed by a German sniper during the Battle of Passchendaele, which cost the lives of more than 300,000 Allied troops. He was not quite 30 years old.

The watch went missing and legend has it that a sniper stole it, which seems highly improbable. Whatever the truth of the matter, the watch was eventually recovered and is now on display at Edmonton Police headquarters. Decoteau was buried in Flanders Field near Ypres, Belgium.

His family never forgot him. Children have been named after him, all pronouncing their name "Alec," as he did. People continue to be inspired by his story. In 2007, The Flanders Athletic Club Ypres and the Memorial Museum Passchendaele 1917 organized an Alex Decoteau Memorial Run in Belgium. Decoteau was inducted into the Sports Hall of Fame of Saskatchewan, Alberta and Edmonton, and was named one of Edmonton's top 100 citizens in 2004.

From 2001 to 2010, an Alex Decoteau Run was held each spring in Edmonton for as many as 1,500 students from kindergarten to grade nine. In the words of his relative, Gerald Wuttunee: "Alex belongs to all of Canada, to all of us and to all the young children."

Historical Photographs

City of Edmonton Archives, EA-302-81

Alex (front, 3rd from left) with runners at the Irish Athletic Club, circa 1908.

City of Edmonton Archives, EA-302-65

Alex (third from left) at the start of a track and field meet at the
Southside Athletic grounds in Edmonton, Alberta, 1915.

City of Edmonton Archives, EA-302-87
The *Calgary Herald* Christmas Day Road Race, 1915.

City of Edmonton Archives, EA 302-74
Alex Decoteau in Emily and David Latta's home on Jasper Avenue,
Edmonton, Alberta, circa 1912.

City of Edmonton Archives, EA 302-82
Alex Decoteau in his policeman's uniform, 1911. Near the Latta home in Edmonton, Alberta, close to the North Saskatchewan River.

City of Edmonton Archives, EA 302-76
Alex Decoteau, 1916, at Sarcee Camp near Calgary, Alberta, where soldiers slept in bell tents. In a letter to his brother-in-law, David Latta, Alex wrote, "I am doing pretty fair in my class as a 'Scout'. Of course I have to work & study hard, but it is so interesting that a fellow doesn't mind."

City of Edmonton Archives, EA-302-73
Edmonton, Alberta, west side of the Latta house. Alex is thought to be wearing a medal he won in a bike race in 1914.

City of Edmonton Archives, EA-302-68
Alex (right), his mother, Dora Pambrun, and a nephew, possibly his brother Alfred's son.

Dora Pambrun, Alex's mother, with some of his many trophies.
Circa 1918, in the Latta home, Edmonton, Alberta.

The Dominion Cigar Store, Edmonton, Alberta, August 3, 1914. A crowd
reads the *Edmonton Journal*'s news of the war, as it is pasted up outside the store.

City of Edmonton Archives, EA-25-41

A house in the Ross Flats (Rossdale). At the end of June, 1915, the North Saskatchewan River flooded. The flood almost washed away the Low Level Bridge in Edmonton, Alberta, which survived because two trains loaded with coal were stationed on the bridge to hold it down. Sergeant Alex Decoteau would have been on duty, helping people escape their homes to the safety of nearby Bennett School.

Bibliography

Awid, Jeff, *Legacy of Heroes: Who was Alex Decoteau?*, Edmonton Police Service, 2014.

Batten, Jack, *The Man Who Ran Faster Than Everyone: The Story of Tom Longboat*, Tundra Books, 2002.

Bishop, Alan & Bostridge, Mark, *Letters from a Lost Generation: First World War Letters of Vera Brittain and Four Friends*, Northeastern University Press, Boston, 1998.

Boyden, Joseph, *Three Day Road*, Penguin Canada, 2005.

Cashman, Tony, *Edmonton: Stories from the River City*, University of Alberta Press, 2002.

Dancocks, Daniel G., *Welcome to Flanders Fields:The First Canadian Battle of the Great War: Ypres, 1915*, McClelland and Stewart, 1988.

Gray, James H., *Red Lights on the Prairies*, A Signet Book, New American Library, 1971.

Gray, John with Peterson, Eric, *Billy Bishop Goes To War*, Talon Books, Vancouver, 1981.

Hallett, Mary & Davis, Marilyn, *Firing the Heather: The Life and Times of Nellie McClung*, Fifth House Publishers, 1994.

Highway, Tomson, *Ernestine Shuswap Gets Her Trout*, Talon Books, 2005.

Keegan, John, *The First World War*, Vintage Canada, 2000.

Little, Joan, *Oh What a Lovely War*, Methuen & Co. Ltd, 1967.

Mair, A.J., *E.P.S. The First 100 Years: A History of the Edmonton Police Service*, Edmonton Police Service, 1992.

McPherson, Arlean, *The Battlefords: A History of the Town of Battleford and the City of North Battleford*, Modern Press, Saskatoon, 1967.

Meili, Dianne, *Those Who Know: Profiles of Alberta's Native Elders*, NeWest Press, 1991.

Meili, Dianne, 'Cree Hero Runs Again: Charlotte Cameron brings Alex Decoteau's Story to the Stage," *Legacy Magazine*, 2001.

Mottershead, Izola, *before – Alex Decoteau – after*, Izola Mottershead, Publisher, Edmonton, AB, Canada, 2004.

O'Shea, Stephen, *An Accidental Historian Walks the Trenches of WW I, Toronto*, Douglas & McIntyre, 1996.

Scott, Canon, *The Great War as I Saw It*, The Clarke & Stuart Co. Limited, Vancouver Canada, 1934.

Stonechild, Blair & Waiser, Bill, *Loyal till Death*, Fifth House Ltd., 1997.

Wasylow, Walter Julian, University of Saskatchewan, *History of Battleford Industrial School for Indians*, 1972.

Acknowledgments

Thanks to my editor, publisher and agent, Morri Mostow, at Fictive Press, who saw a future for the Alex Decoteau story and found a way to keep it running.

Thanks to my husband, Tom Cameron, for taking photos of the rehearsals at the 2001 Fringe, creating props and sets and working so hard to produce and promote the play.

This play is an act of imagination, but it is inspired by real people, archival material, documented dates and events. Many people and organizations gave generously of their time and materials to help me create this play and ensure its historical accuracy. Any mistakes are entirely my responsibility. I would like to thank the following people, and apologize if I have overlooked anyone:

> The late Sergeant Sam Donaghey, the first person to tell me the story and who worked tirelessly to get Alex inducted into the Alberta Sports Hall of Fame and Museum;

> Alex's relatives, Izola and Stan Mottershead, Doug Latta, the late Alex Latta, and Ben DeCoteau, all of whom kept Alex's story alive and shared it with me, providing invaluable information and photographs. Izola Mottershead's 2004 family history, which included letters from Alex, became an invaluable resource. I am grateful for Izola's permission to quote excerpts from Alex's letters to his sister, Emily;

> The late Donna DeCoteau, for her positive energy, introductions to other members of her family, and for her participation in events, such as the trip to City Hall for a presentation to encourage the City of Edmonton to name a street after Alex Decoteau;

> Major (retired) David Haas, Canadian Forces Decoration, JD (Juris Doctor) Royal Military College, director of exhibits at The Loyal Edmonton Regiment Military Museum at the Prince of Wales Armouries Heritage Centre in Edmonton, who provided information and insight into the daily lives of WW I soldiers. In his role as consultant on military matters, he offered advice and suggestions for the 2001 Fringe play, the 2004 family version and, again, for this new Fictive Press version. He also gave permission

to quote from copies of archival materials, such as the Attestation Paper signed by Alex Decoteau and the *War Diary of Lieutenant Colonel Palmer*, and kindly agreed to write the foreword to this book;

The City of Edmonton Police Service, the Edmonton Police Museum and Archives, and the Edmonton Police Foundation;

The National Archives of Canada;

The City of Edmonton Archives for research assistance, access to photocopies of old newspapers, and their excellent collection of photographs;

The *Edmonton Journal* for numerous articles about Alex Decoteau, especially "The Man Who Loved to Run" by Andy Ogle (April 23, 2001).

I also want to thank the following for their invaluable assistance and support:

The Alberta Foundation for the Arts;

Edmonton Public Schools;

Edmonton City Centre Educational Project;

The Edmonton International Fringe Theatre Festival;

Running Room Ltd., for sponsorship and assistance at the Alex Decoteau Runs;

Adrianna Davies, David Ridley and Shazia Sabir, formerly of the Heritage Community Foundation, for developing The Alex Decoteau Edukit website, which can still be accessed online at this archived site: http://wayback.archive-it.org/2217/20101208160721/http://www.edukits.ca/decoteau/index.html;

Pat Cohoon, for her research assistance, and Nina Jackson, for support of the story through her knowledge of heroes as culture carriers;

All the elders, musicians, dancers, guests, principals, teachers, staff, parents and students in the schools that promoted the Alex Decoteau story and participated in the annual Alex Decoteau Runs;

Dianne Meili, broadcaster and author, who wrote a background article about the play, "Cree Hero Runs Again: Charlotte Cameron brings Alex Decoteau's *Story to the Stage*" for the Fall 2001 issue of *Legacy Magazine*;

Heather Inglis of the Alberta Playwrights' Network, for workshopping the play;

Historian Tony Cashman, for his many books and for the personal stories he told me when we were involved with the Fringe Festival;

Laura Roald, Trevor Duplessis, Christine Sokaymoh Frederick, Amelia Maciejewski-Duplessis, Charity Principe, Kurt Spenrath, Joe Procyk, and Dean McQuay, for their support of the story;

White Buffalo Dancer and Drummers Society, and Christine Sokaymoh Frederick.

I am very grateful to my husband, Tom Cameron, our son, Dylan, and his family, and our friends, for their support and encouragement.

About the Author

Charlotte Cameron finds plays an excellent vehicle to retell important stories. She found something so inspiring about the life of Alex Decoteau that she wrote two plays about him. The one in this book premiered at the Edmonton International Fringe Theatre Festival in 2001. Then, thanks to a grant from the Alberta Foundation for the Arts, she wrote a second play, for a family audience, performed on October 8, 2004, for Edmonton's 100th Birthday Celebration in what is now called the Art Gallery of Alberta. It was performed again on November 11, 2004, as a fundraiser for an Early Head Start program, at Alex Taylor School.

Her two other plays, *No Gun for Annie* (2000) and *October Ferries to Gabriola* (2012), also portray real people: Annie Jackson, Canada's first policewoman, and Malcolm Lowry, author of *Under the Volcano*.

Charlotte also enjoys inventing stories, as she did with two published short stories, *Real Cowboys* (*Cumulus*, 1994) and *The Big Bad Wolf* (*Other Voices*, 1994). Her novel, *The Amaranthe*, about the persecution of the Cathars in 13th century France, was shortlisted in the 6th Alberta Writing for Youth Competition.

She has also written profiles for *Legacy Magazine* and articles for *Western Living Magazine*, *BC BookWorld* and *Canada's History*.

Charlotte lives with her husband on Gabriola Island, British Columbia.

Visit Charlotte at fictivepress.com/charlotte-cameron.htm.

CPSIA information can be obtained
at www.ICGtesting.com
Printed in the USA
LVHW101033200522
719304LV00004B/77

9 781927 663134